In One Ear, Out the Other

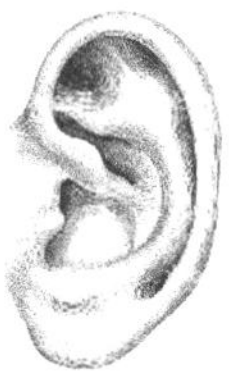

Hearing "The Word" in a

Microwave Society

In One Ear, Out the Other

Hearing "The Word" in a Microwave Society

Ken Bosket

Copyright Information

Collaborative Editing: Kirkus Editing Services

Copy Editor: Dayema Woodall-Bosket

ISBN: 978-0-578-68367-6

Library of Congress Control Number: 2020908690

K&B Information Services Platform

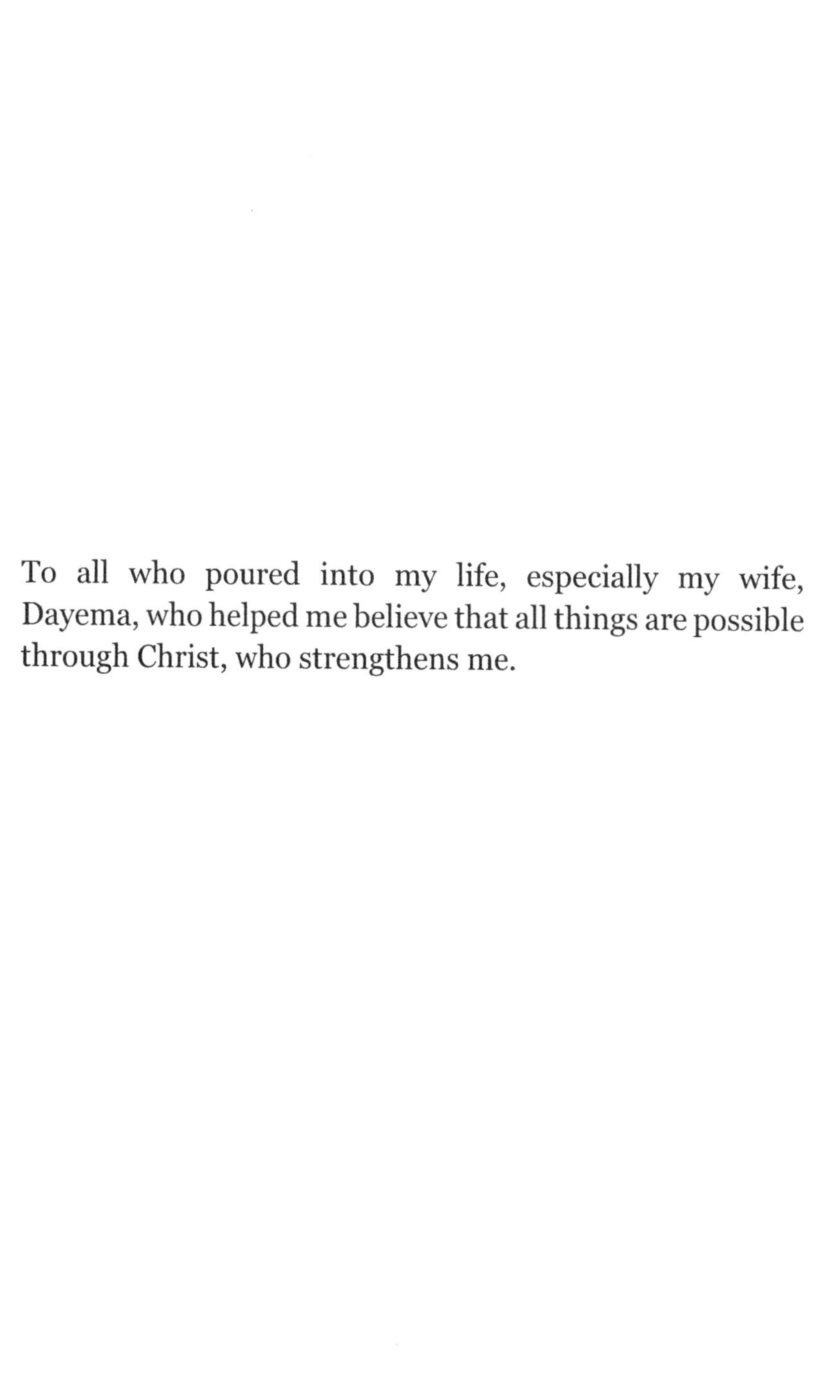

To all who poured into my life, especially my wife, Dayema, who helped me believe that all things are possible through Christ, who strengthens me.

Contents

Preface   11

Introduction   15

Chapter 1: Distractions   21

Chapter 2: Comfortable and Complacent   31

Chapter 3: Discipline and Technology   39

Chapter 4: The Social Media Advantage   47

Chapter 5: Smartphones and the Church   57

Chapter 6: The Influence of Technology   63

Chapter 7: Twenty-Minute Sermon   69

Chapter 8: Does It Ever Really Sink In?   79

Chapter 9: Are We the Problem?   87

Chapter 10: Retain It or Lose It   97

Chapter 11: Hope Is on the Way   107

Chapter 12: The Next Generation   111

Chapter 13: Final Thoughts   123

Generational Timelines   133

Scripture References   134

About the Author   138

"The Word"

In the beginning was the Word, and the Word was with God and the Word was God.

John 1:1

Preface

Has technology gotten out of control in the twenty-first century? Many of us are playing catch-up to an industry that refuses to slow down. Even worse, I believe society has yet to come to terms with the disadvantages associated with this digital culture and the daunting prospects of regulating it.

Is it possible for us to get to a point where the management and regulation of technology can no longer be attained? In a 2017 *Bloomberg* article, physicist and author Mark Buchanan notes that by exploring the negative aspects of today's technology, we can prevent advancing technologies from getting out of control, but because of the speed with which technology is changing, that approach may no longer be effective.[1] The greater part of society readily admits that the advancement of technology can become unmanageable. This issue not only affects civilization as a whole, but also influences every aspect of our personal lives.

So how do we prevent the excessive use of technology from becoming an overwhelming obstacle that might impede our ability to absorb information? This is a critical question, because if we cannot retain knowledge, then how can we trigger any kind of personal transformation, especially spiritual? In the Bible the apostle Paul, who wrote most of the New Testament, addresses this question by stating, "And do not be conformed to this world, but be transformed by the renewing of your mind, that you may

---

[1] Mark Buchanan, "How Technology Might Get Out of Control," *Bloomberg opinion,* August 15, 2017, Bloomberg.com.

prove what is that good and acceptable and perfect will of God" (Rom. 12:2, NKJV).

None of us is perfect, and we all fall short of the glory of God, yet is our humanity an excuse for not disciplining ourselves from the indulgences that come with living in a high-tech society? How can some of us hear scripture week after week and still fail to modify personal and social habits that are not conducive to Christian living?

Is it just our failure to acquiesce to God's standards, or could there be another reason why it is so hard for some of us to adjust our behaviors and discipline ourselves? Perhaps the answer resides in the premise that our increasing exposure to data, in today's "microwave" society (more on this later), has far exceeded our cognitive ability to process it.

I struggle with disciplining myself in today's ever-changing technological society. I face so many disruptions that I find myself failing in my efforts to adjust my lifestyle within this high-tech structure.

The purpose of this book is to have a conversation with you about today's digital culture and its effect on our ability to hear and retain knowledge, particularly scripture. Come and take a journey with me as we explore our capacity to absorb critical information in today's microwave society.

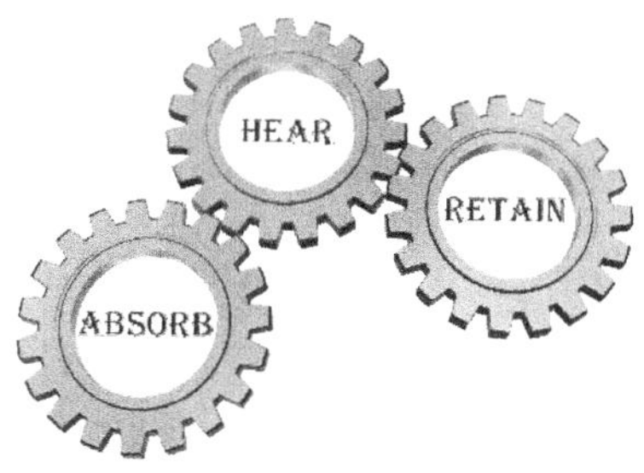

Introduction

Just before the message was preached, Jeff went to the back of the church, as he did every Sunday, to prepare an account for the collected offerings. He, along with four other trustees in his church, diligently counted the money inside every envelope that had been collected. When some change dropped out of an envelope, one of the trustees mumbled aloud, "Look at this [expletive]!" Jeff was stunned and stared at the trustee. He did not expect to hear this type of language coming from a fellow Christian, especially a trustee.

Despite being thrown off his count by hearing this obscenity, Jeff did not say a word. He refocused his mind on the job at hand and continued to count the collections from the service. After the service was over, Jeff was troubled: not only by the trustee's choice of words, but also with the trustee's lack of conviction and acknowledgment of his profanity.

In Jeff's former days, cursing was his second language. The streets were his residence and distributing products (drugs) was his profession. After years of Jeff living on his own terms, God delivered him from a path of drug abuse and criminal activity that was destined to destroy him. Jeff knew he'd been transformed on the inside, and what now resided within reflected on the outside.

This is why the incident at the church bothered him so much. He wondered to himself, "How can a long-standing Christian brother, who faithfully serves God and devotedly supports the trustee committee, curse with such effortlessness?" Without mincing any words the biblical book of Ephesians notes, "Let no corrupt word proceed out of your mouth, but what is good for necessary edification, that it may impart grace to the hearers" (Eph. 4:29, NKJV).

Although the trustee certainly had to know his language was unacceptable, he intentionally continued to count the collected money as though nothing had occurred. That failure to admit wrongdoing bothered Jeff. In hindsight, his sole regret was that he did not respectfully mention the cursing issue to the trustee at that time it occurred.

Absorbing Scripture

What is the difference between hearing, retaining, and living the Word of God? On any given Sunday, inspired sermons are preached with passion to congregations worldwide. Speakers support their messages with scriptures, illustrations and demonstrations, all designed to capture and sustain the attention of their audience. With the influx of today's digital revolution, I believe a more comprehensive, well informed and profound message is being delivered from the pulpit.

Today's practical sermons not only plant seeds in the heart of their hearers but, if retained, can also produce spiritual fruit that can last a lifetime. The biblical book of Matthew uses the planting of seeds as an analogy of a mindset ready to absorb scripture: "The seed that fell on good soil represents those who truly hear and understands God's word and produce a harvest of thirty, sixty or even a hundred times as much as has been planted" (Matt. 13:23, NLT).

Yet with all the Bible applications, commentaries and technical resources available, it can still be difficult for the message to find good soil. The book of Matthew also highlights this concern by stating, "The seed on the rocky soil represents those who hear the message and immediately receives it with joy. But since they have no deep roots, they don't last long. They fall away as soon as they have problems or are persecuted for believing God's word" (Matt. 13: 20-21, NLT).

Is there a chance that the trustee's cursing, along with his failure to admit fault, was really a by-product of spiritual words that had fallen on a rocky foundation? Possibly … or was Jeff asking too much from a fellow Christian who'd been saved by grace and under con-struction like all other

> Yet with all the Bible applications, commentaries and technical resources available, it can still be difficult for the message to find good soil.

Christians? For those of us who may have experi-enced moments of self-righteousness, the apostle Paul stated, "For all have sinned and come short of the glory of God" (Rom. 3:23).

In One Ear, Out the Other: Hearing "The Word" in a Microwave Society explores the subtle and overt issues people contend with as they try to absorb spiritual knowledge in today's high-tech society. Similarly to my book, *Cooked on the Outside, Raw on the Inside: The Struggle to Wait on God's Timing*, a discussion is held in this book about our ability to retain and live God's word in the twenty-first century.

Chapter 1

Distractions

It was Saturday evening and we had just finished working out at the gym. My friends and I were hungry, and our destination was a local diner that was only a couple of minutes away. We sat down at a table and conversed about a host of subjects prior to the arrival of our meals. The engaging discussions and genuine fellowship always kept us coming back for more. What had started out as a spontaneous, after-gym get-together, had grown and evolved into a must-attend weekly event.

Allow me to digress for a moment. I will admit that as technology progressed, I was not prepared for its invasion into my personal space. The rate of speed that computers have become indispensable is over-whelming. The way I see it, the problem with this computer age may be a transitional issue. This digital society has advanced so rapidly that it seems like our culture has not been able to create the ethical boundaries required for technology and humanity to coexist. This is why these Saturday gatherings after the gym were so important to everyone in attendance. It was a way to disconnect from the digital world and embrace the simpler aspects of life. There were no phone calls, texting, email and/or social media. We just enjoyed dinner and the comradery that came along with conversing face-to-face.

> The rate of speed that computers have become indispensable is overwhelming.

A Time and Place for Everything

While waiting for our meals to arrive, I was seated next to a man named John. All of us had known him for years. Whether he was at work or on his own recreational time, he kept his Bluetooth phone unit attached to his ear, engaged and ready for all phone calls. I can understand the need to be in the know, but are not face-to face interactions better than those forged through digital channels?

For most of the evening I ignored John, but as he sat to the left of me on this Saturday, his Bluetooth device was getting me agitated. My problem with these units is that they are so discreet that you never really know if the person is listening to you or conversing with someone else. As predicted, when I turned my head to talk to John, I realized he was speaking on his phone while everyone else was engaged in conversation at the table.

Respectfully, he could have excused himself, but in today's self-centered society, even that would probably be asking too much. It was obvious that he didn't think much about his actions. At some point during his conversation, I just stared at him. He must have felt my frustration because he looked at me, said a few words, then tapped his Bluetooth earpiece to end his call. In essence, I believe we should try to allocate some time in our lives to disconnect from this digital world and enjoy the modest pleasures of life. I can only assume that John would probably disagree with my viewpoint.

Dining Room Disruptions

During its annual convention in 2018, the American Psychological Association (APA) warned attendees that disruptions might occur because of this digital age. Ryan Dwyer, of the University of British Columbia led a 2018 study on digital technology and its effect on relationships. As he noted, "Modern technology may be wonderful, but it can easily sidetrack us and take away from the special moments we have with friends and in person."[2]

Dwyer conducted a study in a dinner setting. He had one set of participants keep their smartphones on the table with their ringers/vibration on, while other participants were told to put their smartphones on silent and in a container.

Similarly to my Saturday-dinner experience, those who had easy access to their phones not only used them more but also felt more distracted and enjoyed the dining experience less. Dwyer surmised the obvious, "People who were allowed to use their phones during dinner had more trouble staying present in the moment."[3]

For some, disruptions can hamper goals, creating a mindset fraught with frustration and discontent. These annoying hindrances, which interfere with our destinies, tend to manifest themselves into major

---

[2] American Psychological Association (APA), *"Dealing with Digital Distraction,"* press releases, August 10, 2018. APA.org.
[3] APA, "Dealing with Digital Distraction."

obstacles that can become barriers to victory. The subtle interruptions that can derail our aspirations and delay our purpose are called "distractions".

Promises, Promises, Promises

It is frustrating when I make a pledge to myself that things are going to be different, only to turn around, evaluate my present circumstances, and see that things are still the same. Why is it that just making a promise to change may not be enough in today's society? How is it that with all the technological advances I have access to, I still feel like I'm playing catch-up with my goals and my purpose? In a digital age full of distractions, a feeling of discontent compels me to come to terms with goals that I have yet to accomplish.

Regardless of my apprehensions and angst, I am aware that I am living in a digital age in which the intake of knowledge is constrained only by the limitations of my mind. The Bible notes the potential for change: "And do not be transformed to this world, but be transformed by the renewing of your mind, that you may prove what is that good and acceptable and perfect will of God" (Rom. 12:2, NKJV). This issue brings me back to my initial thought process, pondering the question of why the process of change seems to be a profound challenge in today's society.

> Why does the process of change seems to be a profound challenge in today's society?

How is it that some of our parents, who had fewer means than we have today, somehow seemed to accomplish far more with less? Digging a little deeper, one might prematurely surmise that the answer could be a lack of willpower, determination or self-control. Nevertheless, many of us have mastered at least one or more of these traits and parlayed them successfully into our personal/professional lives. Perhaps the issue is not an overt problem that can be readily identified, but a covert issue, one in which we engage in the pleasures of this digital age in order to escape the anxieties produced by this digital age. A circulatory process that seems to have no end game.

Should We Be Concerned?

How bad can technological distractions get? On October 24, 2019, in Madrid, Spain, a woman who was distracted by her phone, walked towards the edge of the subway platform and ignored the yellow warning threshold as a train approached. A newspaper article recorded the incident as follows: "The security camera footage shows the unidentified woman using her phone while waiting for the train. As the train approaches the platform, the woman can be seen getting up from her seat and walking right off the edge of the platform. She falls onto the tracks while being distracted by her phone."[4] Most distractions are not as serious as this incident, but technical disturbances, which can unconsciously affect our lives, may not always be noticeable until the damage has been done.

---

[4] *Times Now Digital*, "Woman, Busy on Phone, Falls in Front of Oncoming Train," November 2, 2020, timesnownews.com.

In an effort to protect children, the French government passed a law in 2018 banning all cell phones in schools. In one study published by the London School of Economics, researchers found that students in schools with phone bans in place earned higher test scores, and the lowest-performing students benefited the most. In addition, the researchers wrote, "Study after study shows that the powerful computers, we keep in our pockets, can be distracting for even the most disciplined of adults—not to mention students."[5]

The question now arises: Should we be concerned with the advancement of technology and its ability to distract us from absorbing the word of God? With no computer, internet or smartphone, Albert Einstein, one of the greatest physicist who ever lived stated, "The human spirit must prevail over technology."[6]

Powerful words from the past, foreseeing a future

---

[5] Abigail Hess, "Research Continually Shows How Distracting Cell Phones Are— So Some Schools Want to Ban Them," January 19, 2019, CNBC.com.
[6] Robert Szczerba, "20 Great Technology Quotes," February 9, 2015, Forbes.com.

where the struggle to control technology would be an impending challenge—a perspective that can also be applied to humanities' challenge to hear and retain knowledge in today's digital age. Based on Einstein's assessment, becoming comfortable and complacent with technology may not be a wise choice in today's microwave society.

Chapter 2

Comfortable and Complacent

I was on my way to a technical seminar in Atlanta, Georgia. I had just finished working a long week of trouble-shooting equipment for a major Fortune 500 company. I was on a plane headed to a training that I thought was useless. This was my third year working for this company, and I had just hit my technical comfort zone.

Looking back, my first two years working in the field were chaotic. It appeared as though everything and everyone was working against me. I was new to their system; my manager had no mercy and gave me a territory full of customers. I was theoretically baptized by fire as I struggled to repair equipment throughout my district. I tried to keep a pleasant look on my face, but laboring to restore units to operating condition was a difficult undertaking.

I weathered the storm and after a couple of years, mastered most of the equipment under my jurisdiction. I acquired new trouble-shooting techniques that would help me quickly access a problem, and I learned the necessary communication methods required to deal with customers. I was confident and comfortable with my current work environment.

With that said, I found myself on a plane flying forty thousand feet in the air on my way to Atlanta. I surmised that this training was a setup to add more work to my already-hectic schedule. Once I was certified to repair these new units, I would be responsible for them in the field. I would have to struggle through another learning curve, and I was not ready to endure that type of punishment again.

As the plane landed in Atlanta, my attitude reflected my negative mindset. During the training class, I did not perform well. To top it off, my manager was not happy with the results and, even without me being certified, forced me to work on the new equipment. Wow ... now I was really outside my comfort zone!

Looking back, I should have accepted the training as a way to challenge myself to move outside my area of comfort. Instead, I ended up tarnishing my image with my manager. I was so disturbed by my past learning experience that I was reluctant to do anything other than what made me feel comfortable.

Consequences of Complacency

Just like my experience at work, the drive to be comfortable influences my reason for allowing technology to infiltrate my personal space. We live in a society that has embraced the use of smartphones, tablets, gaming consoles, internet services, mobile apps, social media, etc. But are these sources of convenience a good thing? Even if the long-term effects of digital technology are surmised to be detrimental, are we so far invested in technology that any reduction in its use could be socially and fiscally disastrous?

> ➤ About seventy million Americans regularly listen to podcasts, according to Edison Media Research.

> ➤ In 2019, YouTube reportedly had two billion users worldwide. People watched one billion hours of videos on their platform everyday.[7]

---

[7] Maryam Mohsin, "YouTube Stats Every Marketer Should Know in 2020," November 11, 2019, oberlo.com.

> ➢ More than one billion people use Instagram and more than five hundred million of them use it every day.[8]

> ➢ Nearly three-quarters of Americans (72 percent) are now accessing their bank accounts online and through mobile platforms.[9]

I believe access to technology has allowed us to become so comfortable that our drive to achieve has been somewhat stifled. As a result, some of us have embraced a lifestyle far below God's standards. Unfortunately, our acceptance of this type of mindset may not just be a product of complacency but also a by-product of our fears.

With many of our desires and cravings being fulfilled through digital technology, it's no wonder that some of us are becoming complacent at home, complacent on our jobs, and complacent with our

---

[8]Maryam Mohsin, "Instagram stats," November 29, 2019, oberlo.com.
[9] American Bankers Association, "Mobile are Most Popular Banking Channels," October 16, 2018, aba.com.

spiritual lives. The way I see it, complacency seems to be contrary to the mindset God requires in order to fulfill His purpose.

In the Bible, Abraham appeared to be satisfied with his status until he was called by God at the age of seventy-five to move to another land (Gen. 12:1-3). David seemed to be content with his position as a shepherd, tending the flocks, until he was called by God to be a king (1 Sam. 1-13). At eighty years old, Moses thought he was finally living his best life, until he saw a burning bush that forced him into his destiny (Ex. 3:1-8). The apostle Paul was comfortable imprisoning followers of Christ until he was knocked to the ground and confronted by Jesus (Acts 9:3-9).

> Complacency seems to be contrary to the mindset God requires in order to fulfill His purpose.

A number of us may find ourselves comfortable with complacency. One can speculate that this type of mindset could lead to a false sense of satisfaction. Nevertheless, I believe it is critical that we strive to overcome our tendency to be complacent so that it does not hinder us from achieving God's purpose. Could it be that our best deterrent from comfortability and complacency is to fortify ourselves with a healthy dose of determination and discipline?

"All change begins with a decision. Once the decision is made, discipline becomes the bridge between desire and accomplishment."

Dr. A.R. Bernard – Pastor, Author & Teacher

Chapter 3

Discipline and Technology

One night at the dinner table, I had a discussion with some friends about spending time reading the Bible. Why does it seem like there's never enough time in the day to read and study scripture the way we want to? One individual brought up the fact that he was hindered from reading because he had a problem comprehending scripture. I then told him that I had no excuse for not reading scripture on a daily basis; although I did make one up anyway.

Between my workday schedule and home responsibilities, I occasionally find myself after a long day, getting into bed, saying my prayers and falling to sleep. Even when I do manage to allocate some quality time to spiritual development, scripture is not getting the prime-time attention from me that it deserves. At the conclusion of our meal, we ended our conversation and moved on agreeing that the answer resided somewhere between our strained schedules and our lack of discipline.

Doing the Right Thing

Applying discipline in today's society is a serious undertaking. For the most part, we can get what we want, when we want it. Delay of gratification is not part of the language spoken in our digital age. For those of us who are trying to live a controlled lifestyle, new technologies have introduced new temptations that will require new methods to constrain new habits. The apostle Paul commented on his ability to discipline himself in this way: "When I want to do good,

I don't; and when I try not to do wrong, I do it anyway" (Rom. 7:19, TLB). Paul struggled with doing what was right, even in a first century void of today's disruptions.

Although technology can present difficulties, it can also provide a convenient way to promote discipline. For example, technology allows for the autopay of bills, services and church offerings through banking platforms and online services. This option increases the possibility of making consistent payments in a timely manner. Many of us are content with these types of technological services, but in the end, are they really a good thing? Is the act of having computers implement one's discipline a true benefit or a temporary fix for those who struggle with self-discipline?

> New technologies have introduced new temptations that will require new methods to constrain new habits.

Employing Self-Control

Understanding if technology can be a liability in some circumstances may depend on the access and control it has in an individual's life. Accessibility is a critical term regarding our approach to technology and our ability to filter out excessiveness. Having unlimited access to data unlocks our minds to the best and unfortunately the worst in our society. Even if one is not seeking unethical material on the internet, computer algorithms have a way of monitoring our online activity so that we can be enticed to make poor decisions.

Unfortunately, this is just the beginning. Technology has been advancing so quickly that many of us of us have not developed the control required to override the onslaught. We have websites that encourage husbands and wives to cheat, dating services that deceptively lure people into destructive situations, and internet games that allow children to interact with deceitful adults/predators. How do we discipline ourselves in an unfettered world that seemingly lacks ethics, integrity or decency?

Several of us face this dilemma as we navigate a maze of information bent on taking advantage of our inexperience with filtering data. I believe that I am not alone in my persistent efforts to assert control and time management over a digital engine that refuses to slow down.

So where do we go from here? How do we develop the self-discipline required to move forward? The answer is not simple, but I believe the process starts with prayer. The apostle Paul appeared to confront this same issue. He concluded that he had to take responsibility and control of his life: "But I discipline my body and bring it into subjection, lest, when I have

> It is more advantageous for me to discipline myself, before God has to do it for me.

preached to others, I myself should become disqualified" (1 Cor. 9:27, NKJV).

To look at the situation practically, it is more advantageous for me to discipline myself, before God has to do it for me. I can personally attest that change is not easy. The biblical book of Corinthians validates the need for a personal conversion by declaring, "Therefore, if anyone *is* in Christ, he *is* a new creation; old things have passed away; behold, all things have become new" (2 Cor. 5:17, NKJV).

For some, the challenge to apply discipline in specific areas of their lives is a battle. Combine this struggle with the prospects of invoking change in a high-tech society, and one could be left feeling disheartened and demoralized. Nevertheless, we can be encouraged because the Bible states that we can do all things through Christ who strengthens us. (Phil. 4:13, NKJV).

Despite the challenge to implement self-control, I do believe discipline and technology can coexist today. The question is whether our ability to restrain ourselves and resist distractions is effective enough to overtake an advancing digital era that has no boundaries. When it comes to our capacity to hear and to retain information during this era, only time will tell.

The regulation of technology presents a dilemma, often because of the role social media plays in our lives. But could social media be the main entity that propels Christians into the twenty-first century or is it just another distraction that could hinder us from our spiritual purpose? The conversation continues.

"By giving people the power to share, we're making the world more transparent."

Mark Zuckerberg – CEO Facebook

Chapter 4

The Social Media Advantage

If you ask me whether I am intrigued by the internet and technology, my answer would be yes: addicted ... no. But after being enticed by this indispensable resource, I may have to concede that its unavailability could cause some withdrawal symptoms. After all, the thought of a twenty-first century without all of the technological advances that we enjoy would be inconceivable. This is especially true for the millennial generation, who have witnessed our cultural transition from the analog experience to a digital revolution.

This digital age has not only changed the land-scape of today's workforce, but also transformed the way we enjoy our leisure time. Scanning through sports, entertainment, and news articles keeps me informed, but it also allows me to feel like I am on top of the latest events. Reading opinions articles from "real people," (who would normally not have a voice in traditional news venues) is a welcome dynamic that I relish. Combine these venues with work respon-sibilities, personal assignments, online banking, text messages, emails, and digital socialization, then you may have a formula for internet overdose.

For those of us who love information and data, the internet can be a blessing and a curse. The access to data is amazing and the knowledge obtained through cyberspace is limitless. Websites such as Khan Academy, TED-Ed, Coursera or even YouTube open the door for people to bridge the gap between conventional learning and those seeking a scholastic advantage in today's highly competitive society. Unfortunately, the possible drawbacks from using the internet are its addictive potential and the demands it places on my time. When my leisure time on the internet surpasses my time for spiritual development there may be a problem.

I believe allocating time for meditation and studying God's word allows us to receive spiritual guidance. For example, the Bible provides clarity by noting, "But the Helper, the Holy Spirit, whom the Father will send in My name, He will teach you all things, and bring to your remembrance all things that I said to you" (Jn. 14:26, NKJV). By not managing my time appropriately, is it possible that I could have delayed or missed certain blessings?

> When my leisure time on the internet surpasses my time for spiritual development there may be a problem.

The bishop, filmmaker, and author T.D. Jakes challenged me on the value of time by stating the following: "What do you do when the clock is against you and you have enough wisdom to do it over, but you do not have enough time to do it over? What do you do when you missed your season and you missed your window of opportunity?"[10]

It can be easy for me (and I am sure others) to be caught up in the excesses of this digital age and possibly delay blessings. After all, I can rationalize and justify any of my activities by reminding myself that I deserve some "me" time. As the saying goes, "We work hard so we can play hard." Maybe, but what happens when our playtime inadvertently hinders us from God's purpose?

The Power of a Network

The influence of social media has been extremely effective in shaping today's culture. Social media is

---

[10] TD Jakes, "Nothing Just Happens," YouTube, February 2014.

defined as a form of communication through which users can participate in online communities to share information, ideas, personal messages and other content (such as videos).[11] Some of the more popular social media platforms include Facebook, Instagram, YouTube, Tik Tok, Pinterest, Snapchat, Twitter, and WhatsApp. With approximately 4.5 billion people using digital services daily, social media has become a dominating factor in influencing people to explore the internet.[12]

In 2018, the Pew Research Center found that YouTube and Facebook dominated the social media landscape. That year, the video-sharing site YouTube was used by 75 percent of the adults accessing the internet in the United States. A total of 68 percent of adults who were online used Facebook and 75 percent of those who use Facebook access the site everyday.

---

[11] *Merriam-Webster Dictionary*, "Social Media", on-line edition.
[12] J. Clement, "Global digital population as of January 2020," Statista, Demographics and Use, February 3, 2020, statista.com.

Instagram followed Facebook with 32 percent of all adults accessing its social media platform.[13]

With more than 50 percent of the world's population having access to the internet, there is a tremendous opportunity for Christians to be effective in promoting biblical principles globally. I believe people who incorporate social media into their spiritual outreach may find it to be a valuable resource. Bible studies, prayer groups midweek fellowships, and conference forums are only the tip of the iceberg when it comes to utilizing social media. Social media also allows those who cannot or would not normally step into a church an opportunity

> With having access to the internet, there is a tremendous opportunity for Christians to be effective in promoting biblical principles globally.

---

13 Aaron Smith & Monica Anderson, "Social Media Use in 2018," Internet and Technology, March 1, 2018, Pew Research Center.

to hear the word of God within their comfort zone. Overall, the positive ramifications of using social media seems to be endless.

On March 11, 2020, the World Health Organization declared a virus named COVID-19 (coronavirus) to be a pandemic, a "worldwide spread" of a new disease.[14] In the spring of 2020, Governor Andrew Cuomo of New York declared a state of emergency, banning all public venues from hosting the public. All entities affected by this ban included public settings, theaters, bars, restaurants, concert halls and yes ... churches. Considering this mandate and guidelines coming from the Centers for Disease Control (CDC), some churches decided to connect with their members by way of internet streaming.

During this critical time, the influence of social media was on full display. Those people that were able to take advantage of the technology associated with

---

[14] Jamie Gumbrecht and Jacqueline Howard, "WHO Declares Novel Coronavirus Outbreak a Pandemic," March 11, 2020, CNN Health, cnn.com.

social media were prepared to host critical information for situational/emergency purposes. Because of their recognition of the power of social media, they provided their followers a seamless transition from traditional platforms to streaming services.

The Streaming Machine

The possibility that any individual could at any time reach billions of people around the world is an amazing concept that can have divine implications. By the end of 2020, new smartphone users will account for 66 percent of new global connections, an increase from 53 percent in 2017.[15] Considering the future of mobile devices, the use of social media may be the single most important outreach strategy implemented to advance the Gospel throughout the world.

As more young people accept Christ into their lives, the hope is that they will bring on a heightened sense of spirituality, along with an advanced tech-

---

[15] Rayna Hollander, "Two-Thirds of the World's Population Are Now Connected by Mobile Devices," September 19, 2017, Business Insider.

nological mindset. With that knowledge, they have the potential to go head-to-head with a society that has been inundated with half-truths and misinformation.

In the biblical book of Mark, the example of wine being stored in wineskins (usually made of goatskins) highlights the need for an advanced mindset. As new wine was stored, the fermentation process produced gas, which accumulated and stretched the wineskins. Once the wine was ready for consumption, the old wineskins could no longer be used. If new wine were poured into the old wineskins, its stretched skin would expand even further and burst. Similarly, new wine demands new wineskins, and advanced technology demands an advanced mindset capable of expansion (Mk. 2:22).

New wine demands new wine skins, and advanced technology demands an advanced mindset capable of expansion.

I believe this generation should make a commitment to stay on top of the digital revolution and provide a viable alternative to what the world is offering. With the possibility of six billion smartphone users by the end of 2020, mastering social media may be the bridge that is required for the next generation to hear and retain the Gospel. It's no wonder that faith comes by hearing, and hearing by the word of God (Rom. 10:17, NKJV).

Fifteen years prior to the development of the iPhone, IBM created the first smartphone. What began as a basic means of voice communications evolved into a multifaceted device that altered the way we entirely communicate, interact, and socialize. Our discussion continues as we explore the advantages and disadvantages of using smartphones in the twenty-first century church.

Chapter 5

Smartphones and the Church

One morning a few years ago, while driving to work I realized that I'd left my cell phone at home. I was only five minutes into my commute and had to make a decision. Do I go home and get my phone or do I continue my commute to work? I chose the latter. Besides, I usually receive very few personal phone calls during my workday and even fewer text messages. So why worry if I leave my cell phone home by mistake?

When I arrived at my house later on and looked at my smartphone, I found that I'd received a notification that a bill was due. I had several text messages that required responses. I had friends who wanted to schedule time at the gym, and my wife asked me to bring some food home after work. All of a sudden, a device that was once just a means of verbal communication had become a must-have tool necessary for daily interactions.

Change is Inevitable

Technology has altered everything, especially in the church. I remember seeing my mother respectfully carrying her Bible every Sunday morning. She had a small one that she would take on the go and a larger (jumbo) Bible she displayed on the coffee table at home. I knew not to touch that one!

Today, many congregants have upgraded their physical Bibles to digital Bibles. For some, Bible applications via smartphones have become the primary source of reading and retaining scripture. But is this technological change good for the church? When the congregation uses a physical Bible, everyone's attention is focused on the scripture page. But when they use smartphone Bible apps, one may wonder whether a congregant is reading from the biblical book of John or quietly texting someone named John.

The way I see it, one of the drawbacks of using a smartphone in church is its potential to cause distractions. You can be reading scripture one moment and receiving an email the next. You can be praying in the Spirit one minute and feeling the vibration from a text message (not the Spirit), the next. To be honest, it requires tremendous discipline not to look at your smartphone to see who may be texting you, even during Sunday service.

> The problem with smart phones in the church is not the phone itself but our failure to discipline ourselves from the distractions they may cause.

From my perspective, the problem with smart phones in the church is not the phone itself but our failure to discipline ourselves from the distractions they may cause. Many of us have convinced ourselves that our twenty-four-hour information source cannot be hindered by two hours of church service. This is why many congregants turn their phones to vibrate mode instead of silent or off mode during services. It is a subconscious act enforced by a digital society manipulating many to believe that our connection to the digital highway must not be interrupted, even on Sundays.

How do we begin to disengage from an advancing technology that has so many benefits, but tends to generate distractions that can hinder spiritual growth? A question that presents a dilemma when churches promote the usage of smartphones during services. Many speakers recognize the necessity of technology, but some may wonder whether their audience is actually paying attention.

Are They Listening?

Many pastors encourage note-taking, which is a good thing. At any given time, I can look back on my smartphone and review sermon notes that I typed pertaining to a specific season in my life. But at times I wonder what some speakers are thinking as they talk to their audiences.

In some churches, an intermittent "amen" is appropriate in letting the speaker know that you have heard them. If emotion and the Holy Spirit is moving throughout the church, people raise their hands and stand as the speaker continues his/her message. With smartphones frequently being used during services, do presenters ever wonder whether their congregations are really listening? Maybe they're taking sermon notes with their smartphones.

Perhaps there is something to the process of underlining or highlighting scripture in a physical Bible – an action that can reinforce doctrine in the mind of an individual. But traditional congregants who find smartphones distracting may have to cope as the church continues to incorporate innovative means of technology into its structure.

As this digital age flourishes and the usage of smartphones increases, maybe more people should consider that a widening digital footprint could successfully promote spiritual values. Taking into account the fact that time and resources are major factors in accomplishing this objective, there is no time to waste. Might the influence of technology attract a new generation seeking spiritual identity and hope?

Chapter 6

The Influence of Technology

Not long ago I attended a conference that high-lighted music, technology and production platforms in the church. It was a packed house, and after the initial worship service, the audience broke up into smaller groups. After attending a couple of these meetings a statement made by one of the speakers stuck in my mind. To paraphrase, he stated that the change that churches make to function for the next generation has already made an impact on Sunday services.

That statement stuck with me as I contemplated the adjustments that may have to take place as we progress into the twenty-first century: not only technological changes but also a spiritual mindset open to accommodate the next generation. From what I have witnessed, today's Christian youth appears to be uncompromising and committed. That alone is a good thing. Unfortunately, for some in the church, this radical youth movement comes with worship music that can be intense at best and ear-splitting at worst.

At one well-known church, the volume of the music was so loud that some of the seasoned congregants complained. After much thought and consideration the minister of music came up with a resolution and handed them some earplugs!

Responding to criticism, a renowned international minister stated the following:

People my age are more consumed with what suits them and have lost sight of what we are supposed to bring through; there is an emerging generation coming through … I think older people can decide to move out and watch what God does, or they can make a decision and step in and say I'm going to be a part of what God is trying to do.[16]

Is This Really Necessary?

Just like the musical transitions occurring in some churches, new technologies are rapidly changing the world we live in. Presently, Christians have an opportunity to get aboard the digital train and not be left behind. Some may feel that this venture into technology is moving too quickly and that it requires much thought. Others may

> Christians have an opportunity to get aboard the digital train and not be left behind.

---

[16]Quoted in Pulpit and Pen, "Hillsong Tells Elderly That if They Don't Like Loud Music at Church, They're Selfish and Need to Get Over It," News division, November 26, 2018.

differ and believe the timing is right to stop playing catch-up to a society that is progressively moving forward.

The writer Jonathan Howe, from LifeWay Christian Resources, notes that the utilization of technology around the world is minimal compared to the use of technology in the United States. He states, "Of course, many churches do not use some (or any) of these technological advances. And, honestly, neither your church nor mine really needs any of them to function as a church. Countless churches all over the globe with little to no technology are making disciples in ways that would put to shame some of the most technologically driven churches in the U.S."[17]

I understand Howe's assessment; but as the access to technology advances towards the six billion people mark (there are 7.5 billion people in the world), the internet may be the only viable option available to

---

[17] Jonathan Howe, "What's Next In Church Technology?" Facts and Trends, November 7, 2016, factsandtrends.net.

reach developing nations. With this many people having access to digital technology, Christians should proactively prepare to counter the onslaught of misinformation that can be found on the internet.

Will traditional Christians take the lead in accepting innovative technologies (visual lighting, panoramic video screens, environmental projections, etc.,) as tools that could promote God's word, or will they lag behind a high-tech society that continues to progress forward? Will today's generation concede to the next generation who sees digital technology as an asset to their worship experience? This is an important question because traditional congregants have supported the church consistently and economically for decades. Nevertheless, it is the next generation who will propel the church forward into the future. A delicate balance that requires spiritual insight.

> It is the next generation who will propel the church forward into the future.

The church can play a critical role in disseminating the biblical truths. Houses of worship can provide spiritual balance to a world that seeks answers to critical questions. After all, Jesus did command His followers to: "Go therefore and make disciples of all the nations, baptizing them in the name of the Father and of the Son and of the Holy Spirit, teaching them to observe all things that I have commanded you; and lo, I am with you always, even to the end of the age" (Matt. 28:19-20, NKJV).

By the way, a typical conversation between two people is heard at sixty decibels.[18] I am aware that God may speak in a small voice, but sometimes I wonder, how much of His voice could be heard if worship music is pumping at a whopping 120 decibels! Hmmm ... just a thought.

---

[18] Centers for Disease Control and Prevention, "What Noise Cause Hearing Loss?" cdc.gov/nceh/hearingloss.

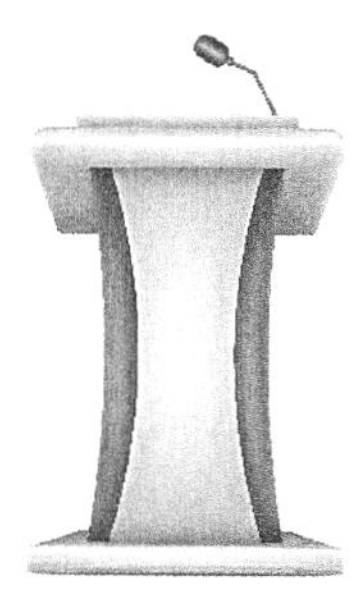

Chapter 7

Twenty-Minute Sermon

It was early Sunday morning and it was time to go to church. My mom made a light breakfast as I put on my Sunday clothes. Now, as a youngster, I was prepared and ready for a full day in church. My morning started with Sunday school, which was held in a little room in the back of the church. Then we took a break. Next were regular church services (no children's church) which lasted throughout the afternoon. Then we would to take another break.

Later we had evening services, which lasted well into the evening. Then I needed a break!

This type of scheduling did not happen every Sunday, but there frequently seemed to be an evening service that would hinder my plans to enjoy the balance of my weekend. It seemed as if the church anniversary, pastor's anniversary, senior choir anniversary, junior choir anniversary, children's choir anniversary, usher board anniversaries, and deacon board anniversaries, all conspired in a scheme to prevent me from enjoying my Sunday-afternoon football games.

As frustrated as I was, I reluctantly grew to respect these programs and traditions as important elements of the church experience. Today, the church has changed significantly. Many of the traditions people hosted when I was a child have faded away—some for good reasons, and some that may not have been for the best.

When I was growing up, the church service was over when the Spirit said it was over. Devotions alone could last forever, depending on how many people wanted to express themselves. Pastors would preach for over an hour and still tell their congregations that they would not be long. There was no air-conditioning in the church during the summer, and to be transparent, as a youth, the best part of the service was the benediction!

Now how can a young man balance out his Sunday schedule, with all these factors getting in the way? Something had to give. Unfortunately, as with some in today's society, as I got older, it was the church and my spiritual growth that got lost in the commotion.

<u>*Time Is Winding Up*</u>

Whether we like it or not, technology has altered the way we process information: 95 percent of families with children, under the age of eight have smartphones, and 42 percent of these same children have access to their own tablet devices.[19] The World Health Organization has expressed concern about the amount of time children spend accessing digital media. This organization is in the process of developing guidelines that may help parents regulate the use of technology with their children.[20] The guidelines may assist a generation who may lack the cognitive and the social-emotional skills necessary to handle critical situations.

A study that included over one million high school students found that teens, who spend more time on screens and less time on non-screen activities like face-to-face socializing, exercise, or homework were psychologically worse off.[21]

How will tomorrow's digital generation come to terms with a forty-minute sermon when their atten-

---

[19] Craig Timberg & Rachel Siegei, "World Health Officials Take a Hard Line on Screen Time for Kids," April 24, 2019, Washington Post.
[20] Timberg and Siegel. "World Health Officials."
[21] Ellen Hendriksen, "How Technology Makes Us Anxious," Psychology Today, March 27, 2018.

tion spans have generationally evolved down to seconds? What procedures must be implemented so that information spoken in tomorrow's microwave society do not go in one ear and out the other?

Speaking to a New Generation

The answer may reside in the twenty-minute sermon. Based on generational trends, I believe the twenty-minute sermon may be a solution as church institutions transition from traditional programs to a platform designed for the next generation. According to the Pew Research Center, the median length of surveyed sermons was thirty-seven minutes. Catholic sermons were the shortest, at a median of just fourteen minutes, compared with twenty-five minutes for sermons in mainline Protestant congregations' and thirty-nine minutes in evangelical Protestant congregations.[22]

---

[22] David Crary, "How long is the Sermon? Study Ranks Christian Churches," December 16, 2019, Associated Press.

With the median length of a sermon concluding in thirty-seven minutes and evangelical sermons finishing in thirty-nine minutes (in my experience more like forty-five minutes), twenty minutes may be all the time speakers have to present their message effectively. Even worse, based on the millennial mindset, speakers have only the first eight seconds of their presentation to capture and retain their audience. This number has decreased from twelve seconds, according to studies conducted in 2000.[23]

> Twenty minutes may be all the time speakers have to present their message effectively.

For those who may feel like they cannot present a deeply insightful message in twenty minutes, Chris Colvin, a research writer who helps pastors write sermons, has noted that some of the most profound

---

[23] David Meltzer, "Combating the Millennial Attention Span to Keep Your Team engaged", October 4, 2017, entrepreneur.com.

passages in scripture, specifically the Sermon on the Mount, could be read aloud in less than fifteen minutes (Matt. 5-7).[22]

Whether speakers like it or not, they are now competing with the new norms of a new society. As someone who is part of Generation X (born 1964 – 1980), I thought I had immunity to the necessity to manage technology. Later, I found out, no one is exempt from the impact of living in this microwave wave society.

It Is Never Too Late to Learn

One day I rushed home from work because I was exhausted and hungry. It was only a matter of time before I ran to the refrigerator and placed my dinner in the microwave oven. Now how many of us can agree that waiting for our dinner to cook in a microwave oven can feel like a lifetime? After staring at the microwave, I had had enough. I stopped the timer, took the food out of the microwave, sat down at the counter, and dug in.

Everything was good up until I cut into the middle of the meat on my plate. It was at that point when I realized that my food was cooked on the outside, but raw on the inside. I don't know why, but at this point I asked myself, "If I can't wait for my food to cook in the microwave, how am I going to wait on a Holy Living God who operates within His own timing?"

During this insightful moment, I decided to write the book, *Cooked on the Outside, Raw on the Inside: The Struggle to Wait on God's Timing*. In the book, I question my ability to wait on God's timing, even if I believed my desires line up with His will.

> I question my ability to wait on God's timing, even if I believe my desires line up with His will.

Whether it is waiting on God's timing or waiting for the completion of a sermon, patience appears to be a required element that is slowly dissipating in today's world. I could be wrong, but twenty minutes may be all the sermon the next generation can absorb as they maneuver their way through an uncharted digital age. Even if speakers succumb to presenting twenty-minute sermons, in a high-tech society inundated by distractions, will any of it really sink in?

"Your self is created by your memories, and your memories are created by your mental habits"

Rick Warren–Pastor, Teacher & Author

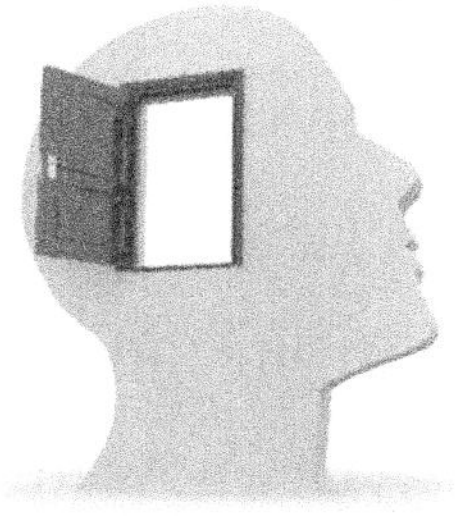

Chapter 8

Does It Ever Really Sink In?

It was a beautiful sunny day for a barbeque, and I was prepared to enjoy it with my family. There was not a cloud in the sky as the sun heated the air to a comfortable seventy-five degrees. I told my sister to text me the location of the event, took a shower, and got dressed for the occasion. The gathering was set in a small township located somewhere in Long Island, New York. I was somewhat familiar with the area, but for some reason I was unable to mentally pinpoint this particular location.

Back when I started driving, there were no GPS devices to navigate me to my destinations. I remember the only way I travelled to unknown locations was to study a map from the American Automobile Association (AAA). We're now in the year 2020. Why should I worry about printing out, retaining or remembering directions for any trip I am planning? As long as there is power in my phone and a navigation application has been loaded, I am good to go. At the end of my journey, the only words I want to hear are, "You have arrived."

After about an hour drive, I finally reached my destination. I greeted everyone that was in attendance, grabbed a chair, sat outside and enjoyed the festivities. Life was good. As evening approached, I wished everyone a good night. If you know anything about the suburbs of New York, as the sun descends, the streets can quickly get dark. On this night, like others, I chose to exercise my memory and try to remember the route home. But after driving around the neighborhood for about ten minutes, I surrendered my ego to technology and decided to use my smartphone for assistance.

I pulled over to the side of the road, entered my home address, and waited for the navigation system to calculate my route. Then I waited a little longer ... and waited a little longer. It seemed to be taking forever for my navigational system to activate. Staring at my phone, I realized that the area I had inadvertently driven into had no signal coverage. I was in what one would call a dead zone.

Now I was in a tough situation. I was lost without a navigational system and phone service. To top it off, I found myself getting deeper in trouble as I continued to drive around, convincing myself that I could find my way back to my cousin's house. In hindsight, I should have paid more attention to some of the street signs I'd passed on the way. I subconsciously heard my wife's voice advising me to print out directions if I would be driving to an unfamiliar destination.

Trusting In Technology

Looking back, I should have known better, but just like everyone else, I had become comfortable with depending on technology. Approximately fifteen more minutes had passed as I wandered in the suburban wilderness. Fortunately, I had a breakthrough as I drove through a neighborhood that had just enough signal coverage to activate my navigation system. I felt relieved as I immediately pulled to the side of the road, locked in my home address and headed home.

In a 2019 *Washington Post* article titled "Ditch the GPS. It's Ruining Your Brain," journalist and author M.R. O'Connor noted the following:

But they [personal GPS devices] also affect perception and judgment. When people are told which way to turn, it relieves them of the need to create their own routes and remember them. They pay less attention to their surroundings. And neuroscientists can now see that brain behavior changes when people rely on turn-by-turn directions.[24]

I used to be very good at creating mental landmarks that would provide guidance and direction while traveling, relying on my visual recollection of stores, restaurants, gas stations and local attractions that I passed on my way. That somewhat dependable technique has been overridden by a technology that thinks for me and subsequently diminishes my natural ability to retain information.

Recollecting the Past

I sometime get frustrated with my inability to recall things. In previous years, I did not have to take notes or use my smartphone to remember simple things. If there was a task that needed to be accomplished, I only had to be asked once, and it was etched in my memory. When I go to restaurants, I marvel at the mindset of servers who can patiently

---

[24] M.R. O'Connor, "Ditch the GPS. It's Ruining Your Brain, Washington Post, June 5, 2019, Washington Post.

listen to my wife and I ramble off our orders, and without writing anything down, get the order completely correct.

My frustration about remembering things is not limited to natural memory loss. I am also referring to people in all age categories who may have become overwhelmed with an increasing barrage of data that must be mentally sifted through on a daily basis. A 2018 study showed that a group pausing to take photos on their smartphones, at regular intervals, had poorer recall of the event than those who were immersed in the experience. Another study suggested that photos helped people remember what they saw, but reduced their memory of what was said.[25]

Catherine Loveday, writer for the *Business Times,* stated that "While it may be true that technology is changing the way we use our memory at times, there is no scientific reason to believe that it reduces the

---

[25] Catherine Loveday, "The Impact of Technology on Our Memory," September 8, 2018, Business Times.

inherent capacity of our brains to learn." Nevertheless, I do suggest that using external devices as opposed to your internal memory can create a dependency issue that can get worse over time.

So how much of the information that we receive in our high-tech society really sinks in? Only time will tell. What we do know, however, is that technology can elicit distractions that can have an adverse effect on our sleep, attention span, and mood. It can also induce anxiety and heighten depression.[26] These symptoms are all factors that can adversely affect our memory.

> Hearing God's word is one thing; allowing His word to penetrate our minds, live in our hearts, and change our ways is another.

Hearing God's word is one thing; allowing His word to penetrate our minds, live in our hearts, and

---

[26] Sarah Barr. "Six Ways Social Media Negatively Affects Your Mental Health," Independent, October 10 2019.

change our ways is another. The apostle Paul challenged us to modify the way we think by stating, "And do not be conformed to this world, but be transformed by the renewing of your mind, that you may prove what *is* that good and acceptable and perfect will of God" (Rom. 12:2, NKJV).

With all the possible distractions we encounter in today's microwave culture, the struggle to stay focused is a critical test that requires discipline so that the knowledge we acquire will not go in one ear and out the other. Are the challenges we face solely the result of a technological infrastructure that is out of control or are we part of the problem?

Chapter 9

Are We the Problem?

Is it possible to have our cake and eat it too? Could a balance be bridged between the onslaught of technology and the needs of humanity? I believe some of us may never develop the discipline required to regulate technology because we're not interested in doing so. Simply put, technology is convenient. They say water will seek the path of least resistance. This is what happens when we employ technology in all aspects of our lives. I surmise that the digital path of least resistance includes any form of technology that has the potential to replace human activities with technological applications.

Computers provide essential services that make most things that were inaccessible, accessible now. But in the end, will this convenience and dependence on technology work out in our interest? Although the underlying effects of computers on humanity are still under evaluation, the advantage of having technology in our lives has created a predicament between what is necessary for us and what is advantageous for us. The apostle Paul notes this dilemma by stating, "All things are lawful for me, but not all things are helpful; all things are lawful for me, but not all things edify" (1 Cor. 10:23, NKJV).

Can we moderately use technology and take advantage of its features without becoming addicted to its benefits? Maybe not. In a 2019 *Washington Post* article, psychologist, author and speaker, Doreen Dodgen-Magee wrote that "technology now reaches deep into our psyches and our lives. Our constant interaction with the digital domain shapes the way we learn, the way we form relationships with others and ourselves."[27]

An Unconstrained Society

Maybe the reason why some of us have issues with regulating our activities is because we have been hooked into an unrestricted digital world that appeals to the good and bad within us. This ideology rationalizes that we should be able to see what we want to see and do what we want to do.

The biblical book of Jeremiah records the instinctive nature of humanity by noting, "The heart is deceitful above all things, and desperately wicked: who can know it?" (Jer. 17:9). I believe we should strive to regulate technology's influence over our lives in spite of our inherited traits. By overcoming toxic aspects of our humanity, we can discipline our

---

[27] Doreen Dodgen Magee, "Tech addiction Is Real. We Psychologists Need to Take It seriously," Washington Post, March 18, 2019.

actions, habits, and behaviors in order to cultivate spiritual growth.

Magee also noted, "The average adult in the United States spends more than eleven hours a day in the digital world, according to research by the Nielsen Company." This means that only thirteen hours are allocated to the balance of one's day. If one gets eight hours of sleep per night, a balance of five hours is left to interact with family and friends. With an average of eleven hours allocated towards digital services, how do we thoroughly refresh our mind so that its capability is not diminished?

> Could it be that we have been hooked into an unregulated digital world that appeals to the good and bad within us?

Performing mental activities that will deconstruct our dependence on technology and constructively stimulate our mind seems to be essential in rebooting our mindset. For example, activities such as reading out loud, mentally working out spelling and math problems, memorizing phone numbers, and driving without the use of a GPS (without getting lost) all assist in preventing one's mental capabilities from declining.[28]

I know these exercises seem a little outdated, but we could learn to occasionally turn away from digital screens and embrace other forms of mental stimulation. As a result, maybe we will develop the mental discipline necessary to regulate the material we take in. By regularly monitoring incoming data, we create a personal filtering process that can decrease or block external distractions. With fewer distractions, we may allow more spiritual growth.

Modifying Our Habits

With the aforementioned focusing on our ability to discipline ourselves, the question now arises, "Are

---

[28] Deane Alban, "Top 15 Brain Exercises to Keep Your Mind Sharp," May 29, 2019, Bebrainfit.com.

we the problem?" The genesis of the problem seems to have begun with the gradual infusion of technology that started decades ago. The successful launch of the digital era required that its infiltration within our culture be slow, meticulous and non-disruptive — a measured process effective enough to generate change yet ambiguous enough to be embraced without apprehension.

Is it possible that we are at a point where the excessive use of technology is so prevalent that its abuse has become normalized? The problem gets exponentially worse when we realize that no regulations can control the actions of those who fail to use their high-tech devices responsibly.[29] One might wonder, at what time in our lives do we begin to blur the lines from the general use of technology to the addictive usage of it. Are many of us on the brink of developing characteristics similar to the addict who

---

[29] Shainna Ali, "Could You Be Addicted to Technology," February 12, 2018, Psychology Today.

consumes too much and still declares that he or she is normal?

In a 2018 article noted in Psychology Today, therapist, educator and author, Shainna Ali states that the "constant use [of technology] has become normalized. The toddler tinkering with a tablet, the teen locked away in their room tied to their computer, and the adult buried in their phone at a social engagement are just a few examples of ordinary use."[29]

<u>Will We Ever Catch Up?</u>

If the excessive use of technology has become the new norm, then how do we apply this standard to our ability to hear and retain God's word? This is a challenging question, because as one develops personal mechanisms to handle the distractions that come with today's digital age, new technologies are being designed to thrust our culture into other technological dimensions. Consequently, we may have to concede that our inability to discipline ourselves may not be just a lack of self-control but a by-product of an advancing technological society that has progressed beyond human capacities. But this doesn't mean that there's nothing we can do.

Self-discipline is effective in mitigating distractions; yet mastering this does not happen overnight. I am not saying that discipline is the only asset we need to discern and regulate our use of technology, but I am stating that it is a significant attribute that is essential for personal growth. Awareness of one's vulnerabilities in our digital world may be the first step in developing habits that can modify the way we approach technology.

> The development of self-discipline is a process that does not happen overnight.

So are we the problem when it comes to hearing and absorbing the word of God in this microwave society? My initial response was no. But I do believe that we contribute to the problem by not acknowledging and correcting personal factors such as, lack of focus, restraint, and self-control.

Now that we discussed the importance of maximizing our ability to absorb information, how do we ensure that the information taken in is preserved? It would be a shame hear "The Word" and not be able to recall it. In Chapter 10, we will look into the possibility that what we cannot retain, we could lose.

"Sometimes you will never know the value of a moment until it becomes a memory"

Dr. Seuss – Author, Illustrator

Chapter 10

Retain It or Lose It

Most of the time, my weekday morning routine is consistent. On this one morning, however, things had quickly spiraled out of control. When I look back, I really do not know what happened. My alarm clock was set for 6:00 a.m., as it was every morning. Because of the tight timeline I have in the mornings, I had completed most of my preparations the previous night. Prior to bed, I had verified the alarm settings on my smartphone.

My upcoming morning would be a little different from the others. I had an important meeting to attend, and I needed to be prepared and on time. Therefore, when I heard the alarm at 6:30 a.m. instead of 6:00 a.m., I panicked. I was still half-asleep as I stumbled my way to the bathroom. Now it was 7:00 a.m., and I was already thirty minutes behind schedule. I rushed to get a half-hour process done in a few minutes. Finally, after some hustle, my clothes were on, my morning essentials were done, and I was ready to go.

Hurrying to put my coat on, it came to my attention that I did not have my glasses. The time was now 7:30 a.m., which was a major problem because if I could not find my glasses, then I would not be able to drive to work. After looking for my glasses for fifteen minutes, I had had enough. It was now 7:45, and I was done. I paced the kitchen floor, looked up at the ceiling as though it was all God's fault, and shouted, "What is going on?" As I raised my hand to wipe my eyes, I felt my glasses sitting right where they were supposed to be ... on my face! I could not believe it.

I shook my head in disbelief as I grasped the reality that my glasses had been in my possession the entire time (do not judge me: just laugh). After pacing the kitchen floor in astonishment, I tried to rationalize this bizarre incident.

Maybe it was the breaking of my morning routine or the possibility of doing too many things at one time. Perhaps I was distracted by so many things that I put the glasses on without being conscious of it. These were the only answers I could come up with that made sense. I will admit that my ability to remember things is not what it used to be.

Triggering Our Memory

Information retention is defined as having data stored in long-term memory in such a way that it can be easily retrieved.[30] Initiating the process for knowledge to be transferred from short-term memory to long-term memory is one issue; triggering a process that will allow long-term memory to release the data upon demand is another story. Women, however, appear to have a distinct triggering advantage over men, especially when it comes to recall.

Doctor, author, and pastor of the Christian Cultural Center, A.R. Bernard, has clarified the issue:

> Women can recall the details: we [men] can only recall the headlines. A woman simply has to get in touch with her feelings. In other words, she has to first recall the emotions she experienced at the time of the event, and once she makes the connection with that emotion, all the data comes flooding back into her mind, putting the man at a disadvantage.[31]

---

[30] A.G Bennett and N.S. Rebello, "Retention and Learning," *Encyclopedia of the Sciences of Learning*, Springer, springer.com.
[31] A.R. Bernard, "Message: Special Guest, Dr. A.R. Bernard," Zoe Christian Fellowship of Whittier, October 13, 2019, YouTube.com.

Looking back at the chaos that ensued that morning, not only was there no triggering process on the whereabouts of my glasses, but as I researched this phenomenon, there seemed to be an issue with a process called "encoding." Without being technical, let us dig a little deeper into this term.

The encoding process begins with the way we perceive things. Once we are conscious of an image or event, our minds take in (encodes) all the separate but distinct characteristics of the visual image we are observing. Our brain then collects all the components that make up what we see and creates one visual experience that can be stored in our memory.[32]

It still bothers me that I could not remember that I had picked up my glasses and placed them on my face. I now understand that my inability to recall the location of my glasses may not have been the result of a faulty memory. It may have been because of my

---

[32] Richard Mohs, "How Human Memory Works," How Stuff Works.

mind's failure to encode all the information required to recall the whereabouts of my glasses.

Breakdown in the Process

With that being the case, what can cause an interruption in the brain's ability to encode events? In an article on how memory works, Chief Scientific Officer for the Global Alzheimer's Platform Foundation and author Richard C. Mohs wrote that "distractions that occur while you're trying to remember something can really get in the way of encoding memories. If you're trying to read a business report in the middle of a busy airport, you may think you're remembering what you read, but you may not have effectively saved it in your memory."[33]

Could it be that the encoding process went awry because my mind was distracted? Maybe. Distractions seems to block the encoding process by hinder-

---

[33] Richard Mohs, "How Human Memory Works."

ing the brain from gathering all the data required to develop an image.

So how do we retain knowledge so that we can grow both mentally and spiritually? The first way, as previously noted, is to eliminate unnecessary distractions that may hinder us from taking in information and storing it. This is critical because if we can't focus on scripture and retain it, then how will we be able to develop the spiritual values God has for our lives?

Another way to retain knowledge is to practice the process of "mind association." In order to remember a specific image or person, one can associate that image or person with a distinct sound or graphic, which can then be easily stored and recalled by the brain.[34] A practice that can contribute to the recollection of scripture by associating scripture with unique incidences. The more personal the experience, the more likely we will remember specific scriptures.

---

[34] Psychologist World, "Memory and Association," psychologistworld.com.

This can be very effective during seasons of our lives when it's crucial to recall God's word.

A third way to store data into long-term memory is repetition. Repetition leads to reinforcement, which is essential in transferring data from the encoding process to long-term memory. Repetition can also lead to the development of routines that can be beneficial in developing spiritual consistency. For example, reciting scripture repeatedly can benefit one's ability to recall passages that can promote spiritual development.

It is good for some of us to know that a moment of forgetfulness is not a permanent issue, but a temporary matter that can be mitigated with repetitive drills, mental activities and cognitive exercises.

Age Is Not a Factor

For those who are concerned about the ability to recall information as they get older, studies show that the aging process does not necessarily coincide with memory loss. Mohs noted, "Studies also have shown that many of the memory problems experienced by older people can be lessened or even reversed. The important point to remember is that as you age you may not learn or remember as quickly as you did when you were in school, but you will likely learn and remember nearly as well."

That is good news for those who strive to absorb and retain data in this microwave society. Even if our ability to retain information is somewhat impaired, the outlook still looks bright as we welcome a future generation accustomed to recalling data despite technical distractions. "Let not your hearts be troubled …" (Jn. 14:1), hope is on the way.

"Hope is being able to see that there is light despite all of the darkness"

Desmond Tutu–Bishop, Nobel Peace Prize

Chapter 11

Hope Is on the Way

So where do we stand as a culture and community in regulating the forces that adversely affect our ability to retain information? For many, retaining information in the twenty-first century has become a challenge, stemming from an advancing technology that generates undesirable distractions. Recognizing this dilemma, society has conceded that we are playing catch-up to an evolving digital culture.

This is not to negate the significance of today's technology. The new technological freedom many of us have experienced has led to the development of new processes, abilities, skills, and associations that have radically changed our lives for the better. The way I see it, however, humanity is currently engaged in a struggle with itself as accessibility, comfort, and convenience clash with an undisciplined society gradually spiraling out of control.

Our hope begins with a millennial generation and their acceptance of a technical revolution that has changed the digital landscape of the world. Who are the people who make up the generation we call millennials? According to the Pew Research Center, anyone born between 1981 and 1996 is considered a millennial, and anyone born from 1997 onward is part of a new generation called Generation Z.[35]

---

[35] Michael Dimock, "Defining Generations: Where Millennials End and Generation Z Begins," January 17, 2019, Pew Research Center.

Millennials are the key to thrusting our society into the digital age. They were open to innovation and accepted the possibility of a digital revolution that could culturally transform society. Their acceptance of change has led to the development of a computer infrastructure that has invaded the fabric of our world. Although the millennial's acceptance of technology is unparalleled, they have still struggled to handle the distractions that have arisen with this new paradigm. If millennials are the forerunners of technology, then Generation Z are the generation called to continue their legacy.

> Millennials are the key to thrusting our society into the digital age.

Rising to the Occasion

Generation Z (born 1997 – 2009) were born into technology, fed off technology and put to bed with technology. Because of their birthright, they have developed the innate ability to multitask technology while naturally negating distractions. Their potential is promising, and their ability to embrace technology is reassuring. Their capability of sustaining a disciplined lifestyle in an emerging digital world is an asset that prior generations do not possess.

Looking at the situation practically, we find that our future relies on an emerging generation. But God always has a plan. The scriptural book of Psalms records God's purpose for our lives: "This will be written for the generation to come, that a people yet to be created may praise the Lord" (Ps. 102:18, NKJV). It is encouraging to know that God will always provide a way, even if He has to fulfill His purpose through the next generation.

Chapter 12

The Next Generation

I was recently in a store looking for a printer. It had been ten years since I'd purchased my last printer, and my knowledge on the subject was antiquated at best. Talk about advancements in technology. There were so many printers, with so many options, that even I, as a techie, had to step back and compose myself. After a lengthy period of time researching printers on my smartphone, I gave up. The over-whelming quantity of data was too much for me to take in. In frustration, I dropped my ego and asked a customer service representative for help.

While I waited for the representative, I already had my guard up as I struggled to cram and retain as much knowledge as I could before he arrived. I was aware that he was working for the store and was most likely looking to sell me what he wanted me to buy. I'd been down that road before and did not want to go there again.

As the representative approached, he shook my hand and introduced himself as Brandon. After a brief dialogue, Brandon began his presentation and spoke knowledgeably on the advantages of each printer. He asked me whether I would use the printer in my home or in a work environment. He inquired about whether I needed a standard printer or a multifunction/all-in-one unit. He noted the benefits and disadvantages of purchasing an inkjet printer rather than a laser printer.

Finally, near the end of his presentation, Brandon rattled off a host of supplemental information that drove my mind into data overload. Enough was enough! I asked him how he was able to learn and retain all the information he had detailed for each brand of printer. He smiled and told me that he was self-taught and had learned everything he knew about printers from personal experience and on the internet.

Talk about bridging the digital divide. Even if traditional learning platforms fails to produce quality educational programs, this digital age has provided a non-traditional learning resource that has the potential to close the gap between the haves and the have nots. Amazed with his motivation, I commended him on his ability to seek the knowledge required to be competent in his current position. The conversation then seamlessly shifted from printers to life skills. He looked young enough to be a millennial, and I was curious about his mindset as we entered the year 2020.

A Lesson from a Millennial

Brandon had graduated from the University of California and was currently working at an office supply store for income. He aspired to be an information technology (IT) manager and was waiting for an opportunity to achieve his goal. Just from my initial conversation with this young man, I felt good about the next generation.

Our conversation continued for well over an hour. He seemed eager to speak about his objectives and I was willing to hear his story. As Brandon spoke about the opportunities available in his field, I recommended that he apply for positions at smaller companies to gain some IT experience and then go for the career position at the corporation he had been dreaming about. It made sense to me.

At that point Brandon looked at me, thought about what I was suggesting, and said, "Why would I want to do that? I need to be comfortable." I stared at him perplexed and politely asked him to repeat his statement. With no hesitation he stated, "I need to be comfortable." In confusion, I realized that I might have just been hit with a millennial moment. Glaring at him for a second (I needed some time to think), I respectfully responded, "Sometimes you have to work your way up to be comfortable, and the truth be told, even then, there's no guarantee that comfort will be part of your work environment."

Brandon just looked at me as though I were speaking in another language, and after an awkward pause, he smiled. Sensing an uncomfortable moment, I changed the topic back to printers. After a few more minutes of conversation, I gave him a fist bump, commended him on his knowledge and told him that I was rooting for him. As I walked out the door, I shook my head, feeling technically informed on one hand and generationally confused on the other.

A Change In the Workplace

According to the 2016 Dell & Intel Future Workforce Study Global Report, 56 percent of millennials that year believed that advanced technology leads to more productivity in the workplace. The embracing of innovative technologies would allow employees more time to focus on creative thinking, human exchanges and value-added work (appreciated work resulting in a complete product).[36]

By adding these ideals to a workplace's environment, the emphasis on production would include practices that respect and embrace an employee's values. Could this be the reason why Brandon was adamant that comfort would be a major factor in choosing a place of employment? I thought his vision was a little shortsighted, but in an economic structure, where quality workers are a limited commodity,

---

[36]Mike Beels, "What is Value Added vs. Non-Value Added Work?" Michigan Manufacturing Technology Center, February 8, 2019, the-center.org.

employers may have no choice but to accommodate the demands of millennials and ensuing generations.

The Bigger Picture

If this is a mere snapshot of the millennial mindset within today's workforce, then what about the forthcoming generation. I am talking about a generation who is just entering the workforce and already placing demands on it. A generation who sincerely believes that today's labor force will concede to their desires for comfort. Unlike their predecessors, they are motivated by workplace security, not just money.

In a 2017 Forbes article, entrepreneur, marketer and best-selling author, Deep Patel wrote that "Gen Z has been living in a world of smartphones and free Wi-Fi for as long as they can remember. Ninety-two percent of them have some sort of digital footprint. Their relationship to technology may be even more instinctual than that of a millennial in their late 30s."[37]

Whereas millennials transitioned into a digital age, Generation Z was born into a digital age. Even more important, members of Generation Z have mastered the world of multitasking. They were born into a digital society full of distractions. Based on Patel's article, I presume that they have developed instinctive coping mechanisms that allow them to disregard distractions. Unlike millennials and the generations before them, Generation Z may have the advantage of adaptability on their side.

> Whereas millennials transitioned into a digital age, Generation Z was born into a digital age.

Patel noted this advantage by stating that "These young people have always lived in a connected world,

---

[37] Deep Patel, "8 Ways Generation Z Will Differ from Millennials in the Workplace. September 21, 2017, Forbes.com.

and they're used to constant updates from dozens of apps. Switching between different tasks and paying simultaneous attention to a wide range of stimuli comes naturally to them." While millennials and other generations before them were easily distracted by the onset of technology, members of Generation Z have inherently developed a firewall that allows them to focus on their goals despite the presence of disruptions.

This is a critical asset, because if future generations are to hear and retain information in this microwave society, they must manage distractions. Generation Z's ability to focus and exhibit control over disturbances is an indispensable quality. This progressive functioning is necessary for the twenty-first century.

The Future Is Here

Just like the advancement of technology, we must be prepared to embrace the succeeding generation. As authors Adrienne Pasquarelli and E. J. Schultz note,

"Barely out of diapers, they're already playing an outsize role in household buying decisions. Born beginning in 2010, the same year Apple debuted the iPad, these children are more comfortable swiping a tablet or speaking to a voice assistant than most of their adult relatives."[38]

This next generation arriving after Generation Z is quietly waiting to place their mark on society. They are expected to be able to hear, absorb, and retain more information than any past generation. Their effect on the distribution of the Gospel will be critical as they adopt, embrace, and introduce new forms of technology. Their expected lifespan will far exceed the lifespan of any of their predecessors, and with God's grace, they will be the most technologically advanced generation that ever lived.

God's commitment and foresight referencing future generations was biblically recorded well before

---

[38] Adrienne Pasquarelli and E.J. Schultz, "Move Over Generation Z, Alpha Is the One to Watch," January 22, 2019, Adage.com.

humanity became technically savvy: "And I will establish my covenant between me and you and your offspring after you throughout their generations for an everlasting covenant, to be God to you and to your offspring after you." (Gen. 17:7, ESV).

Welcome Generation Alpha; born 2010 - present!

"Never before in history has innovation offered promise of so much to so many in so short a time."

Bill Gates – Microsoft Corporation

Chapter 13

Final Thoughts

Together we have explored the subtle and overt issues we have to contend with as we try to absorb and retain information in our fast-paced society. We have now arrived at a juncture in our conversation where we must ask a critical question again. Has technology gotten out of control in the twenty-first century? For Generation X (born 1965 – 1980) and millennials, the answer appears to be a reluctant … yes.

Currently, many in our society have struggled to create boundaries with a technology that provides comfort and generates complacency. Experts assert that regulating the progression of technology may be an unmanageable task. Moreover, the struggle to create boundaries not only involves technology by itself, but also human will.

> With smartphones in their hands and bibs around their necks, they have been fed digital milk since birth.

By the end of 2020, new smartphone users will account for 66 percent of new global connections, up from 53 per-cent in 2017.[39] This increase in smartphone usage, along with the development of more appli-cations, will revolutionize the way people interact in the twenty-first century. With that said, the question now arises: Will we take the lead in

---

[39] Hollander, "Two-Thirds of the World's Population."

adopting more technology into our church platforms, or will we rely on the next generation to lead the way?

Natural Born Leaders

Born in the year 2010, members of Generation Alpha (zero to ten years old in 2020) have the benefit of growing up with a twenty-first century mindset. With smartphones in their hands and bibs around their necks, they have been fed digital milk since birth. In a 2019 article published in *Business Insider*, Ashley Fell, director of communications at McCrindle Research stated that "they have been wired all of their lives ... this generation is part of an 'unintentional global experiment, in which screens are placed in front of children at the same time as pacifiers."[40]

Nevertheless, it is expected that Generation Alpha and beyond will have the ability to master the latest technologies far more than their predecessors. Their ability to absorb information and make decisions in

[40] Ursula Perano, Axios. "Generation Alpha is tech-heavy and extremely connected," August 8, 2019. Business Insider. businessinsider.com

spite of the chaos around them will be a welcome asset in a complex world. They will have the potential to expand the technical boundaries of the church so that its outreach will remain an effective resource.

Whereas millennials and Generation Z have embraced the progression of digital technology, Generation Alpha may be the hope for tomorrow as technology advances into a digital era besieged with the latest robotics and sophisticated technologies. During this generational shift, God reminds us that He is directing our paths: "But I have raised you up for this very purpose, that I might show you my power and that my name might be proclaimed in all the earth" (Ex. 9:16, ESV).

> Generation Alpha and beyond will have the ability to master the latest technologies far more than their predecessors.

Minimizing Technical Distractions

With this generational transition taking place, today's society still has to bridge the gap between our personal productivity and our insatiable appetite for technology. Therefore, relying on your brains instead of your smartphone for the little things can be effective in breaking the technology habit. Here are some other suggestions that may be helpful in overcoming distractions.[41]

- ➤ Create a technology-free environment in which all electronic devices are set aside for a specific time of the day. This is a good way to reduce one's dependence on technology.

- ➤ Turn off or limit smartphone notifications. This can be effective in reducing the desire to respond to every beep or chime the phone emits.

---

[41] Fizzle. "10 Ways to Cut Internet Distractions So You Can Focus on What Really Matters," August 15, 2017, fizzle.co/sparkline/cut-internet-distractions-focus-really-matters.

➤ Relocate the most frequently used apps from the main page of the smartphone to another area that you don't use frequently. As they say, out of sight, out of mind.

➤ Use the clock and calendar app to set alarms and reminders for important assignments and activities. This will allow you to focus on a schedule.

➤ Make use of timers to manage the time spent on specific tasks.

Looking Into the Future

As I watch my nieces and nephews (Generation Alpha) constantly gazing into their smartphones and iPads without any regards for their surroundings, I sometimes wonder whether the experts and pundits are correct. From my narrow vantage point, Generation Alpha seem to be self-absorbed in a world that is out of touch with reality. Nevertheless, empirical studies assert that they are part of a much-needed generational shift that is on the way, one that will create a new paradigm that I believe will embrace the technological and spiritual growth of humanity.

Balancing the Use of Technology

We evaluated the impact distractions can have on our ability to retain information. We also have a greater understanding on how our personal initiatives can be stifled when we become comfortable and complacent. Despite the challenges we face, discipline seems to be the key to offsetting technology distractions that can hinder our spiritual growth.

> I sometimes wonder whether the experts and pundits are correct.

Whether it is in the church or in our homes, devices such as smartphones play a major role in how we communicate and interact with people. Although there may be some ethical concerns with the role smartphones play in facilitating social media, they can be very effective in promoting the Gospel globally.

With the next generation on the horizon, Christians may have to accommodate youth whose attention span is limited to seconds. This is significant because if speakers/presenters do not understand the inherited digital mindset of the next generation, how can their messages soak in and be effective?

> If speakers/presenters do not understand the inherited digital mindset of the next generation, how can their messages soak in and be effective?

It is the forthcoming generation that will pick up where previous generations left off. By balancing their use of technology with time allocated for spiritual development, upcoming generations have the opportunity to spread "The Word" to an unrestricted digital society.

With all the technological advances and distractions that can occur in the twenty-first century, I believe our current challenge is to remain spiritually mindful as we discipline our actions so that "The Word" will not go in one ear and out the other.

God bless.

"It has become appallingly obvious that our technology has exceeded our humanity"

Albert Einstein—Noble Prize in Physics

Generational Timelines

Baby Boomers: 1946 - 1964

Generation X: 1965 - 1980

Generation Y (Millennials)

1981 – 1996

Generation Z: 1997 – 2009

Generation Alpha: 2010 - present

Pew Research Center

Scripture References

And do not be conformed to this world, but be transformed by the renewing of your mind, that you may prove what is that good and acceptable and perfect will of God (Rom.12:2, NKJV).

Let no corrupt word proceed out of your mouth, but what is good for necessary edification, that it may impart grace to the hearers (Eph. 4:29, NKJV).

The seed that fell on good soil represents those who truly hear and understands God's word and produce a harvest of thirty, sixty or even a hundred times as much as has been planted (Matt. 13:23, NLT).

The seed on the rocky soil represents those who hear the message and immediately receives it with joy. But since they have no deep roots, they don't last long. They fall away as soon as they have problems or are persecuted for believing God's word" (Matt. 13: 20-21, NLT).

I can do all things through Christ who strengthens me (Phil. 4:13, NKJV).

But my God shall supply all your needs according to His riches in glory in Christ Jesus (Phil. 4:19, KJV).

For the good that I will to do, I do not do; but the evil I will not to do, that I practice (Rom. 7:19, NKJV).

But I discipline my body and bring it into subjection, lest, when I have preached to others, I myself should become disqualified (1 Cor. 9:27, NKJV).

Therefore, if anyone *is* in Christ, he *is* a new creation; old things have passed away; behold, all things have become new (2 Cor. 5:17, NKJV).

But the Helper, the Holy Spirit, whom the Father will send in My name, He will teach you all things, and bring to your remembrance all things that I said to you (Jn. 14:26, NKJV).

All things are lawful for me, but not all things are helpful; all things are lawful for me, but not all things edify (1 Cor. 10:23, KJV).

This will be written for the generation to come, that a people yet to be created may praise the Lord (Ps. 102:18, NKJV).

But I have raised you up for this very purpose, that I might show you my power and that my name might be proclaimed in all the earth (Ex. 9:16, ESV).

So shall my word be that goes out from my mouth; it shall not return to me empty, but it shall accomplish that which I purpose, and shall succeed in the thing for which I sent it (Isa. 55:11, ESV).

For I know the thoughts that I think toward you, says the LORD, thoughts of peace and not evil, to give you a future and a hope (Jer. 29:11, NKJV).

Let not your heart be troubled; you believe in God, believe also in Me (Jn. 14:1, NKJV).

About the Author

Born in the projects of New York City, Ken Bosket uses the challenges of life as a platform for his current success. Always thinking, Ken questions the norms of society and inquires about whether today's mindset can be effective in tomorrow's high-tech culture. Concerned with his efforts to balance his personal and spiritual goals in today's digital society, Ken's curiosity challenged him to evaluate the sometimes-conflicting relationship between humanity and technology. Without any previous writing experience, Ken expressed his thoughts on paper and wrote his first book, *Cooked on the Outside, Raw on the Inside: The Struggle to Wait on God's Timing,* in 2018. In an effort to keep his books reader-friendly, he developed a writing style that is light-hearted, inquisitive, informational and thought provoking.

AVAILABLE ON AMAZON

In One Ear, Out the Other

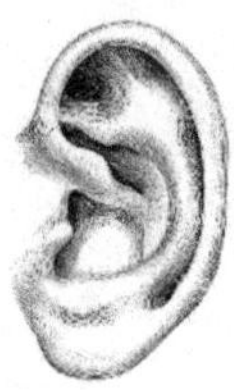

Hearing "The Word" in a

Microwave Society

www.kenbosket.com

www.cookedontheoutside.com

cookedontheoutside@gmail.com

Notes

Made in the USA
Monee, IL
07 July 2026